Jesus and the Fishermen

This

Bible Story Time book

belongs to

____

____

____

Text by Sophie Piper

Published by
Lion Hudson Limited
Wilkinson House, Jordan Hill Business Park,
Banbury Road, Oxford OX2 8DR, England
www.lionhudson.com

ISBN 978 0 7459 6360 0
e-ISBN 978 0 7459 6813 1
ISBN 978 0 7459 7855 0 (pack of 10)

First edition 2006
This edition 2014

A catalogue record for this book is available from the British Library

Printed and bound in China, April 2019, LH54

Bible Story Time

Jesus and the Fishermen

Sophie Piper * Estelle Corke

LION CHILDREN'S

Jesus grew up in Nazareth.

Like everyone else, he went to the synagogue each week.

He listened as the teacher read from the holy books.

He listened as the teacher talked about God.

When Jesus was a man, he became a teacher too.

People from other towns asked him to come and teach in their synagogues.

He read from the holy books.

He talked about God and God's love.

More and more people wanted to hear what he had to say. Jesus began to spend every day teaching.

One day, Jesus was teaching by Lake Galilee. Lots of people came to listen. The people at the back couldn't see him.

Jesus saw two fishing boats on the beach. "Please let me use a boat," said Jesus to the fishermen. "I'll get on, and you push it into the water. Then everyone will be able to see me."

At the end of the day, Jesus called to one of the fishermen. "Simon, come and let the fishing nets into the water. You and your friends will catch a lot of fish."

"No we won't," said Simon. "We didn't catch any last night."

"Try," said Jesus.

They caught more fish than the nets could hold.

Suddenly, the fishermen felt rather scared of Jesus. "I don't think I'm good enough to be your friend," said Simon.

"I want all of you to be my friends," said Jesus. "You're very good at gathering fish in nets. I need you to help me gather people: people who want to be part of God's family."

The fishermen came: Simon and his brother Andrew; James and his brother John.

Later, Jesus chose eight more people to help him, making twelve special friends.

Jesus and his friends often went by boat. It was a good way to get to other towns beside Lake Galilee.

Jesus wanted to teach in lots of places.

One evening, Jesus and his friends set off by boat.

The fishermen were in charge of sailing it.

Jesus went to lie down with his head on a pillow. Soon he fell asleep.

In the night, a strong wind began to blow.

It blew the water into waves.

The wind and the waves tossed the boat. Jesus' friends were very scared.

"Wake up, Jesus! Wake up!" they cried. "You've got to help us or we'll die."

Jesus stood up in the boat.
He spoke to the wind:
"Be quiet!"
He spoke to the waves:
"Be still!"

At once, the lake was calm.

"Why were you scared?" asked Jesus. "Do you not have faith in God?"

The eight friends looked at the four fishermen. “Did you think it was a scary storm?” they asked.

“Yes,” said the fishermen. “But not as scary as what Jesus just did.”

They all began to wonder the same thing: Who can Jesus be? How can he do miracles like that?